Original title:
Distant Fields

Copyright © 2024 Swan Charm
All rights reserved.

Author: Johan Kirsipuu
ISBN HARDBACK: 978-9908-1-2200-7
ISBN PAPERBACK: 978-9908-1-2201-4
ISBN EBOOK: 978-9908-1-2202-1

The Call of Untraveled Trails

Beneath the sun, adventure gleams,
Whispers of wander in silver streams.
Paths yet untread beckon anew,
Joyous laughter, the sky so blue.

Each step ignites a spark of delight,
Winding and twisting, both day and night.
With friends beside, we'll chase the sun,
Together we'll sing, for life's just begun.

Dancing with the Wind's Embrace

Soft breezes tease the sunlit air,
Twilight's fingers weave golden hair.
Laughter spills where shadows play,
The rhythm of joy shines bright today.

With hearts alight, we spin and twirl,
In nature's ball, our spirits swirl.
Each gust of wind, a vibrant cheer,
In this dance of life, we hold so dear.

Forgotten Pathways

Leaves crunch gently beneath our feet,
Every corner hides a new heartbeat.
Memories float on the autumn's breath,
In silence, echoes of joy and death.

We wander through the maze of time,
In every moment, a whispered rhyme.
With each step forward, we reclaim the past,
A journey of love, forever to last.

Horizon's Gentle Lament

As daylight fades, the stars ignite,
An open canvas of dreams, so bright.
Whispers of night call us to roam,
In twilight's arms, we find our home.

The horizon beckons with a soft sigh,
Each shade of dusk a lullaby.
Together we wander, hearts intertwined,
In this fleeting moment, peace we find.

When the Sun Sets on Memory

Golden rays dance in the sky,
Children laughing, spirits high.
Stories shared on evening breeze,
Laughter mingled with rustling trees.

Candles flicker, shadows play,
Heartfelt moments on display.
Under stars, dreams take flight,
Memories glow with soft twilight.

Nature's Lonely Reverie

Petals drift on gentle streams,
Nature sighs in whispered dreams.
Bees hum sweetly, lives entwined,
In this realm, pure joy we find.

Mountains stand in noble grace,
Secrets kept in time's embrace.
Festive colors burst anew,
Every leaf a vibrant hue.

Scraps of Sky and Soil

Kites soar high on summer's breath,
Life and laughter free from death.
Picnic blankets spread with cheer,
Precious moments drawing near.

Fields of gold beneath the sun,
Every heart feels young and fun.
Joyful voices rise and swell,
In this place, all is well.

Whispers of Faraway Shores

Waves crash softly on the sand,
Children build with eager hands.
Seagulls cry and fly so free,
In this scene, pure harmony.

Sunsets spill on ocean's face,
Fleeting time, a warm embrace.
Festive laughter fills the air,
Peaceful hearts, without a care.

Hues of a Harsh Sun

Golden rays stretch wide and bright,
Laughter dances in the light.
Balloons soar with every cheer,
Joyful hearts draw loved ones near.

Children play in summer's glow,
Faces painted, smiles in tow.
Sipping drinks with vibrant hues,
The sun sets, we share our views.

Music fills the evening air,
Rhythms beat without a care.
Festive lights begin to shine,
In this moment, lives entwine.

As twilight wraps the day in bliss,
Each shared laugh feels like a kiss.
Moments cherished, memories spun,
Underneath the hues of sun.

Uncharted Waters of the Mind

Sailing deep through thoughts unbound,
Waves of wonder swirl around.
Each direction holds a key,
Unlocking dreams, wild and free.

Colors merge in vibrant tides,
As the spirit freely glides.
In this realm, the heart will roam,
Charting paths that feel like home.

Echoes drift on gentle winds,
Stories told as laughter spins.
With each splash, the soul ignites,
A festive dance on endless nights.

Together we embrace the ride,
On these waters, side by side.
In the depth, we find our way,
Creating joy for every day.

In the Quiet of the Afternoon

Sunbeams filter through the trees,
Soft murmurs flow upon the breeze.
A picnic spread, laughter flows,
In the quiet, friendship grows.

Colors bloom in scattered light,
Dandelions, pure and bright.
Blankets laid on blades of green,
A festive scene, a cozy sheen.

Time slows down, as moments blend,
Every smile, a loving trend.
Behind the veil of nature's song,
Together here, we all belong.

As the day begins to wane,
Golden hour, a soft refrain.
In this space, we find our tune,
Basking 'neath the watching moon.

Linger of an Old Song

Melodies drift through evening skies,
Whispers soft as fireflies.
Rhythms pulse like heartbeats true,
Every note, a memory new.

Gathered close, we hum along,
In the air, an ancient song.
Voices blend, a vibrant hue,
In this moment, we renew.

Laughter echoes, spirits soar,
As nostalgia opens doors.
Footsteps dance on cobblestone,
Underneath the stars, we're home.

In the linger, time stands still,
Festive hearts beneath the thrill.
With every beat, we find our place,
An old song holds us in its grace.

Tapestry of the Sky and Earth

Colors dance in evening light,
A canvas bright, a joyous sight.
Laughter rises, spirits soar,
In every heart, a vibrant core.

Stars are stitched with threads of gold,
Stories shared, and dreams unfold.
Underneath the moon's sweet gaze,
We celebrate these fleeting days.

Petals swirl with fragrant grace,
In the warmth, we find our place.
With friends and family near,
We craft memories year by year.

Together in this festive cheer,
A bond that grows, sincere and dear.
As the night wraps us in its glow,
We treasure each moment, let love flow.

The Gaze of Faraway Thickets

Whispers of leaves in the breeze,
Soft shadows dance among the trees.
In every rustle, joy ignites,
A symphony of nature's rights.

Children laughing, voices clear,
Chasing dreams without a fear.
In the thickets, secrets shared,
A world of wonder, wholly bared.

Butterflies flit on sunny trails,
Painting paths where laughter sails.
The branches sway, our hearts align,
In this haven, all is divine.

With every moment we embrace,
We find our rhythm, our true place.
Festive hearts, like birds in flight,
Together soar into the night.

Up the Gentle Slopes of Memory

Step by step, we climb the hills,
Each memory sparks, a bright thrill.
Nostalgia sings in the golden glow,
As laughter echoes, soft and slow.

Trees whisper stories from the past,
Moments cherished, memories vast.
We gather blooms of sweet delight,
Under the blanket of starlit night.

In every corner, tales unfold,
Of friendship, love, and hearts of gold.
As shadows lengthen, and stars align,
We share our dreams like vintage wine.

On these slopes, time stands still,
Every heartbeat, a joyous thrill.
In the warmth of the festive air,
We find our truth, we find our care.

Landscapes Lost to Time

In the dusk, where memories play,
Old landscapes breathe a soft array.
Colors fade, yet spirits shine,
In the heart, they intertwine.

Faces of laughter, stories shared,
Echoes of moments, lovingly bared.
Through fading light, we hold on tight,
To the bonds we forged in the night.

A tapestry woven of joy and tears,
In every thread, we conquer fears.
Though some may fade into the past,
The festive spirit forever lasts.

So here we gather, hand in hand,
Celebrating life, a glorious band.
In the embrace of love's warm glow,
We dance through time, let our friendships grow.

Invisible Tides of Memory

Laughter dances in the air,
Echoes of joy we all share.
Stars above twinkle bright,
Guiding us through the night.

Fireflies weave through the gloom,
Whispers of magic softly bloom.
Each moment a spark, a dream,
Flowing like a sweet, gentle stream.

Songs of old begin to play,
Reminding us of yesterday.
Together we bask in the light,
In the warmth of shared delight.

Memories woven, thread by thread,
In the tapestry of what we've said.
Invisible tides that bind us near,
Crafting a story, year by year.

The Grace of Open Spaces

Fields of green stretch far and wide,
Where sunbeams and shadows collide.
Laughter echoes with every breeze,
Nature sings amidst the trees.

Open skies, a canvas blue,
Painted with dreams, old and new.
Every flower, a burst of cheer,
Whispers of joy draw us near.

Picnics spread on soft, warm ground,
In every corner, joy is found.
Moments shared in peace and bliss,
Life's simple pleasures, we won't miss.

Evenings glow with golden hue,
As the stars unfold their view.
In open spaces, our hearts take flight,
Together dancing in the night.

Canvas of the Shifting Sky

Clouds blush pink with the setting sun,
A masterpiece when day is done.
Brushstrokes of gold reflect our cheer,
As daylight fades, stars appear.

Twilight whispers secrets untold,
In hues of violet, crimson, and gold.
Every glance toward the endless dome,
Illuminates a dream of home.

In the twilight's soft embrace,
We gather warmth, a sacred space.
Hearts aligned with the universe,
In this moment, our souls converse.

The night sky, a canvas vast,
Bringing joy from the present and past.
We paint our hopes with starlit smiles,
As we wander the cosmic aisles.

Stray Thoughts in the Meadow

In the meadow, laughter sways,
Dancing lightly on sunlit rays.
Wildflowers nod in gentle cheer,
Drawing us close, year after year.

Children's giggles fill the air,
Chasing dreams without a care.
Butterflies flit, a vibrant show,
Time suspended, as soft winds blow.

Kites soar high, colors ablaze,
Marking moments in a joyful haze.
Each heartbeat pulses with delight,
Wrapped in the magic of the night.

In the meadow, stray thoughts roam,
Finding comfort, making this home.
Together we celebrate, side by side,
In this haven, where dreams abide.

A Solitary Journey

The lanterns glow along the path,
Each flicker sings a silent laugh.
Footsteps dance on cobbled stone,
In whispers sweet, I'm not alone.

The night is young, the stars so bright,
Their twinkling hearts ignite the night.
With every turn, the world feels right,
A solo cheer in soft moonlight.

As laughter swirls through every street,
I find the rhythm, feel the beat.
The echoes of joy resonate,
In every corner, love holds fate.

Though journeyed far, my heart stays near,
In every smile, in every cheer.
Together here, though miles apart,
A solitary song fills the heart.

The Golden Echo of Silence

In fields of gold beneath the sun,
The laughter of children has begun.
A soft breeze carries tales of grace,
With every moment, joy we chase.

The quiet hum of nature's song,
In stillness, where the heart belongs.
Golden echoes reach the skies,
They softly kiss the evening's rise.

Beneath the shade of whispering trees,
We share our dreams on gentle breeze.
A warm embrace of love and light,
In silence, everything feels right.

As sunset paints the world anew,
The golden hues in every view.
We gather close, in joy, we thrive,
In golden echoes, we come alive.

Sighs from the Wilderness

Through rustling leaves and twilight's gleam,
The wilderness hums a vibrant dream.
With every sigh, the forest breathes,
In nature's arms, the spirit heaves.

A dance of shadows, whispers flow,
Where wildflowers sway and rivers glow.
The serenade of crickets sings,
In wild delight, the heart takes wings.

The stars emerge, a glistening view,
In the embrace of night so true.
Together we wander, hand in hand,
In this wild world, we make our stand.

With every pulse of earth beneath,
A love for life, in peace, we sheath.
The sighs that rise from every tree,
In wilderness, we roam so free.

Beneath the Weight of Time

In moments paused, we savor light,
As laughter dances, hearts take flight.
Beneath the stars, our dreams unfold,
In stories shared, life's joys retold.

With every heartbeat, time flows sweet,
In every soul, the warmth we greet.
The whispers of ages softly call,
In unity, we rise, we fall.

Candles flicker, shadows play,
In gentle comfort of the day.
With every glance, a promise made,
In love's embrace, all fears will fade.

Together we stand, as seasons change,
In memory's heart, we're not estranged.
Beneath the weight of time, we find,
In every moment, love intertwined.

Shadows of the Wandering Wood

In the wood where shadows play,
Twinkling lights dance in the fray.
Laughter rings among the trees,
Joyful whispers on the breeze.

Golden leaves in swirling flight,
Moonlit paths that feel so bright.
With every glance, a secret shared,
In this realm, all hearts are bared.

Beyond the River's Embrace

Where the river's laughter sings,
Gathered friends with hopeful wings.
Picnic blankets on the shore,
Food and stories we adore.

Bubbles rising to the skies,
Sunset hues in joyful sighs.
With every splash, a memory,
In this place, we are so free.

The Silent Call of Open Spaces

In the fields where daisies stand,
We unite, hand in hand.
Kites soar high with colors bright,
Chasing dreams into the light.

Whispers of the wind so clear,
Every laugh brings those we cheer.
Here the world feels vast and wide,
In open spaces, we confide.

In Search of the Unseen Horizon

Beneath the stars, our wishes flow,
Guided by the dreams we sow.
Adventurers with hearts so bold,
In the night, our stories unfold.

With each step, the journey calls,
Echoing joy as twilight falls.
The unseen horizon whispers true,
A festive spirit shining through.

A Spiral of Fading Light

In twilight's glow, the lanterns sway,
Whispers of laughter fill the day.
Colors dance on the breeze so light,
Hearts are lifted, spirits bright.

The stars awaken in velvet skies,
Glimmers of hope in every eye.
We twirl and spin with joy in sight,
In this magic, we take flight.

As shadows play their fleeting game,
Each moment calls, will never tame.
With friends beside and dreams in sight,
We chase the spark of fading light.

So let the night embrace our song,
For where we're free is where we belong.
In this laughter, hearts unite,
In the spiral, the world feels right.

Embrace of the Endless

Underneath the arching trees,
The music flows on gentle breeze.
Gathered here in joyful cheer,
We welcome love, we welcome near.

With every tune, our spirits rise,
Echoes of laughter touch the skies.
Hands entwined, we sway and reel,
In every heartbeat, warmth we feel.

Radiant moments, bright like gold,
Stories of friendship, forever told.
In this circle, we find the light,
An embrace of the endless night.

So raise a glass to dreams we share,
To vibrant hearts that deeply care.
In this festivity, pure delight,
We dance together, hearts ignite.

Rustling Pages of an Untold Tale

In the corner, where shadows dwell,
A story whispers, soft as a shell.
Pages rustle, secrets unfold,
Adventures waiting, brave and bold.

Ink spills dreams beneath the stars,
Fables of hope, healing scars.
Gathered close, we listen tight,
To tales that shimmer in the night.

With every laugh, a new chapter grows,
In every pause, the magic flows.
Together we weave this ancient thread,
In the rustling pages, joy is bred.

So turn the leaf, let stories soar,
With every heartbeat, we crave more.
In this festivity, tales ignite,
In the night, our dreams take flight.

The Language of Withered Petals

Withered petals dance so free,
Whispers of a jubilee.
Colors fade but hearts still sing,
Joyful memories they bring.

In the breeze, they swirl around,
Spreading laughter, soft and sound.
Each drop of color, bright and bold,
Stories of love silently told.

Gathered in a gentle throng,
Life's sweet chorus, vibrant, strong.
Underneath the twilight shade,
New delights in dusk are made.

So let the petals drift and sway,
In the cheerful light of day.
Their language speaks in every hue,
A celebration, bright and true.

A Fable in the Breeze

Beneath the stars, tales unfold,
A fable in the breezy cold.
Moonlight glimmers, soft and sweet,
As night wraps us in its sheet.

Whispers float from tree to tree,
Nature's secrets, wild and free.
Fireflies blink their lights in sync,
Like laughing stars on the brink.

In the shadows, joy takes flight,
Every heart beats pure and bright.
Together by the candle's glow,
The stories of the night will flow.

In this magic, we find peace,
The festive spirit won't cease.
So let us revel in this night,
As our dreams take wing in flight.

Glide of the Evening Star

The evening star begins to gleam,
A shimmering and hopeful dream.
Dancing lightly through the sky,
Wishes floating, sweet and shy.

Underneath the vibrant hues,
People gather, share their views.
Laughter mingles with the air,
Joyful spirit everywhere.

With every twinkle, stories weave,
Bonds of love that we believe.
In the warmth of friendship's glow,
Hearts united, spirits flow.

So when the stars begin to play,
Let our troubles drift away.
For in this wondrous cosmic dance,
Life's sweet magic finds its chance.

Soft Shadows of the Past

Soft shadows whisper through the trees,
Painting memories in the breeze.
Echoes of laughter fill the night,
As we gather, hearts alight.

Underneath the silver glow,
Stories from long ago we sow.
Each gentle flicker of the flame,
Filling the air with love's sweet name.

In this moment, time stands still,
Festive joy that we can feel.
Every shadow holds a tale,
Binding us in friendship's veil.

So let us cherish these delights,
As we bask in warm, soft lights.
For in each laugh, in every glance,
We weave together our own dance.

Whispers of the Horizon

Golden rays dance on the waves,
Joyful laughter fills the air,
Children's games and vibrant hearts,
All is bright, free from care.

Balloons float up to the sky,
Colors swirl, a painter's dream,
In the moment, time stands still,
Life's a joyful, flowing stream.

Candles flicker in the breeze,
Sweets and smiles on every face,
Underneath the twilight glow,
We embrace this sacred space.

As the stars begin to shine,
Fireflies twinkle like the hope,
Whispers of the night unite,
Together, we learn to cope.

Between the Meadows and Clouds

Fields of daisies waving high,
Butterflies flit, a gentle cheer,
The sun is warm, the sky is bright,
Nature's song is all we hear.

Breezes stir the fragrant air,
Picnics laid on blankets wide,
Laughter mixes with the song,
In this joy, we take pride.

The brook babbles, a sweet tune,
Reflecting moments, pure and free,
Hand in hand beneath the trees,
Life feels endless, a jubilee.

As clouds whisper their secrets low,
We revel in this festive hour,
Together we find our way home,
United in love's warm power.

The Promise of Forgotten Valleys

Hidden gems in the sunlit glen,
Whispers of joy from long ago,
Echoes of laughter softly call,
In these valleys, memories flow.

Petals scatter in the breeze,
Colors painted on the earth,
Joyful gatherings around the fire,
Celebrating life, its worth.

Nature wraps us in her arms,
As we dance 'neath the twilight glow,
Each moment cherished, every smile,
The promise of bonds we sow.

Through the valleys, hand in hand,
We weave our stories, strong and true,
In the heart of this festivity,
Our dreams dare to break through.

Echoes Over the Pastures

Through the hills and golden fields,
We gather close to celebrate,
The laughter bounces, the music plays,
Filling hearts, it's not too late.

Bonfires crackle, warmth surrounds,
Stories shared with every glance,
In the twilight's enchanting grip,
We twirl and laugh in a dance.

Songs of old and dreams anew,
Resonate across the night,
A tapestry of joy is spun,
As stars above shine ever bright.

In echoes soft, our spirits soar,
Connected in this festive cheer,
Together, we'll face tomorrow's dawn,
With laughter, love, and no fear.

Where the Heartbeats Slow

Where laughter dances in the air,
With joy and music everywhere.
The lanterns twinkle, bright and bold,
A warmth like stories yet untold.

Together we share this cherished space,
With smiles that time cannot erase.
The gentle whispers of the night,
Turn every shadow into light.

As hands entwine, the worries fade,
In this embrace, our hearts parade.
The world outside feels far away,
In moments here, forever stay.

Beneath the stars, we sing as one,
In every heartbeat, life's sweet fun.
With souls aglow like candle flames,
Together we weave these vivid aims.

The Sound of Far-off Bells

In the distance, bells do chime,
A melody that feels like rhyme.
Their echoes blend with laughter near,
Inviting all to gather here.

Each note a step on pathways bright,
Guiding us through this joyful night.
With every ring, the spirits soar,
And paint the air with tales of yore.

As friends unite beneath the light,
We're drawn together, hearts so bright.
The sound of bells, like whispers sweet,
Calls forth a dance that's pure and fleet.

So let us raise our voices high,
To celebrate beneath the sky.
With every chime, embrace this cheer,
In this grand moment, hold it dear.

Wandering Roots

We wander paths where laughter flows,
In gardens where the wildflower grows.
The vibrant colors kiss the sun,
In nature's arms, we find our fun.

The earth is rich with tales entwined,
Of restless hearts and dreams defined.
As every step stirs joy anew,
We trace the roots of love, so true.

With every breeze, whispers of joy,
In every leaf, there lies a story.
The branches dance with gentle grace,
Inviting us to find our place.

Each moment spent, a treasure stored,
As wandering souls grow ever bored.
Together here, the world feels vast,
In blooming fields, we are steadfast.

Palettes of a Fading Glow

The sunset spills its colors bright,
As day turns slowly into night.
With brushes dipped in gold and rose,
The canvas whispers as it glows.

Awash in hues that gently blend,
With every stroke, the day will end.
Stars emerge in twilight's embrace,
A tapestry of time and space.

As laughter dances on the breeze,
We gather close among the trees.
With every cheer, the night ignites,
In festive hearts, the magic lights.

So let us paint with memories dear,
In palettes rich, where all is clear.
With faded glow, our spirits rise,
In every moment, love defies.

Fields of Faded Dreams

In golden fields where laughter sings,
Children dance on fragile wings.
Colorful kites in skies so bright,
Whispers of joy in the soft twilight.

Beneath the trees where shadows play,
Smiles abound, and worries sway.
With each shared tale, the night unfolds,
Festive spirits, as warmth beholds.

Gifts of friendship in the cool breeze,
Memories woven through vibrant leaves.
A banquet laid for hearts to cheer,
Toasts of hope and dreams we steer.

As stars above begin to gleam,
We celebrate this faded dream.
Hand in hand, we stride as one,
Under the glow of the softening sun.

A Tapestry of Distant Stars

In the velvet sky, a canvas bright,
Threads of silver, woven light.
Each twinkle holds a secret song,
Inviting all to join along.

Gathered close beneath the moon,
Together we hum a soft tune.
As laughter echoes through the night,
The tapestry glimmers with delight.

Stories drift like fireflies' glow,
Sharing dreams that gently flow.
In the boundless night, we dare to dream,
A festival of hopes, a radiant theme.

With sparks released to touch the stars,
We send our wishes, near and far.
In this moment, we truly see,
A tapestry of unity.

Threads of a Vanished Landscape

In a landscape where colors blend,
Threads of memories never end.
The air hums with a joyous call,
As we gather for the evening ball.

Sunset spills its golden grace,
Painting smiles on every face.
With each note of our merry song,
The past and present weave along.

Laughter dances like flickering lights,
While friendship warms the chilly nights.
In this tapestry of heartfelt cheer,
We celebrate all we hold dear.

As shadows lengthen, time stands still,
In our hearts, we feel the thrill.
Threads entwined in a soft embrace,
A vanished landscape, yet we find our place.

The Last Breath of Summer

In petals blooms the summer's sigh,
With every breeze, a whispered goodbye.
Golden rays paint the skies so wide,
As we cherish these moments, side by side.

The laughter rings through fields of gold,
In every story, a memory told.
Underneath the dancing trees,
We savor the warmth of gentle ease.

As twilight beckons with a cool embrace,
We gather close in this cherished space.
With hearts alight, we bid adieu,
To summer's hush and skies so blue.

Yet in our hearts, the warmth will stay,
As we celebrate this fleeting day.
The last breath of summer, pure and sweet,
In sharing joy, our lives complete.

The Essence of an Unfamiliar Horizon

Bright colors dance in playful light,
A tapestry woven, a dreamy sight.
Laughter echoes in the warm breeze,
As hearts embrace this gentle tease.

Joyful voices rise to the sky,
Celebrations twinkling, oh so high.
Each moment savored, a treasure found,
In this blissful world, love knows no bounds.

Serenade of the Swaying Grasses

Whispers of nature in the soft air,
Grasses sway gently, a rhythmic flair.
Beneath the shade of a grand old tree,
We gather together, wild and free.

Strings of laughter, a melody sweet,
Dancing around in the warm summer heat.
Fingers entwined in a joyful embrace,
Time stands still in this cherished space.

Secrets of the Untraveled Path

Hidden wonders along the way,
Bright blossoms bloom where shadows play.
With every step, a new delight,
We chase the stars into the night.

Luminous fireflies, a guiding spark,
Illuminating paths that once were dark.
Together we wander, hearts aglow,
In this enchanted land where magic flows.

Valleys Painted in Solitude

Soft whispers wrap around the hills,
Where nature's breath forever thrills.
Golden hues splash the evening sky,
While time drifts gently, oh so high.

In places quiet, yet alive,
The spirit dances, dreams revive.
With every heartbeat, a pulse so bright,
Solitude sings of pure delight.

Moonlit Promises

Under a sky of shimmering light,
Laughter dances, hearts take flight.
Joy weaves through the whispering trees,
Embracing warmth in the evening breeze.

Stars twinkle like secrets shared,
A night of dreams, beautifully paired.
With every promise made tonight,
We celebrate love in the silver light.

Candles flicker, casting soft glow,
Brightening paths where friendships flow.
Toasting to moments stitched with glee,
In the moonlit realm, we feel so free.

With each heartbeat, the night unfolds,
Tales of happiness, laughter retold.
In this tapestry, joy interlaced,
Moonlit promises, forever embraced.

Footprints in Forgotten Soil

In fields where memories sway and sing,
Footprints linger, a joyful spring.
Echoes of laughter, the past awakes,
In harmony with each breath that breaks.

Under the arches of ancient trees,
We gather stories with every breeze.
Through vibrant colors, our spirits play,
In the soft light of a fading day.

Winds carry whispers, secrets anew,
Tracing paths where friendships grew.
Together we stand, in moments profound,
Painting our dreams on the hallowed ground.

As twilight beckons, the stars appear,
In this shared silence, there's nothing to fear.
With every step, there's magic embraced,
In the footprints of love, forever traced.

Ephemeral Odes to Yesterday

Moments flutter like petals in flight,
Dancing through shadows, kissed by light.
We sing to the echoes of days gone by,
In the festival glow of a twilight sky.

Memories woven in laughter and cheer,
Resounding joy that lingers near.
With every heartbeat, we cherish the now,
As ephemeral odes take a solemn bow.

With each sunset, there's beauty reclaimed,
A celebration of all that we've named.
In the warmth of remembrance, our spirits soar,
Festive and bright, forevermore.

So raise your voice, let the music play,
For yesterday's treasures light up today.
In fleeting moments, let love intertwine,
In an ode to the past, our hearts align.

The Stories We Left Behind

In the twilight glow, the tales unfold,
Of laughter and dreams, both brave and bold.
With each passing hour, we gather and share,
The stories we left, with love in the air.

Through winding paths where we used to roam,
In every memory, we find our home.
Echoes of joy in the softest of sighs,
Reminding us gently where true treasure lies.

Fires glow bright, as shadows weave,
Of the hopes and wishes we dared to believe.
In the warmth of the night, our souls intertwine,
Celebrating lives that forever shine.

As the stars gather, and the moon climbs high,
Our stories unite, beneath the vast sky.
With every retelling, we honor the glow,
The stories we left behind still flow.

A Mosaic of Forgotten Lands

Beneath the skies, so vast and bright,
Colors dance in joyful light.
Each piece a story, bold and grand,
A vibrant tale of distant lands.

Echoes of laughter fill the air,
As dreams and memories freely share.
With every step, a spark ignites,
In this mosaic, heart takes flight.

Festooned trees in emerald hues,
Whispering secrets in gentle clues.
The spirit of joy, we weave and twine,
In this tapestry, life's divine.

Banners of hope in the breeze sway,
Celebrating life in a grand array.
With every heartbeat, we dance and sing,
In this festive realm, our hearts take wing.

Reverence of Nature's Reach

In the cradle of blooms, nature sings,
Of sunlit paths and fluttering wings.
Every petal a dream, each leaf a tale,
Embracing the beauty where wonders prevail.

Golden rays through branches peek,
Nature's embrace tender and meek.
In the rustling leaves, a laugh rings true,
In the arms of the Earth, we start anew.

Footsteps soft on the carpeted ground,
In serene silence, joy is found.
The rhythm of life, a sweet refrain,
In nature's embrace, we rise again.

Beneath the stars, we gather near,
With hearts full of hope, we cast out fear.
The festival of life unfolds with grace,
In reverence, we dance in this sacred space.

When Time Embraces Solitude

In quiet corners, shadows play,
Time whispers soft, then slips away.
A gentle pause in life's swift chase,
Embracing solitude's warm embrace.

Each moment stretches, crisp and clear,
In stillness found, the heart draws near.
With every breath, a blissful sigh,
In solitude, we learn to fly.

Sunset hues wrap the world in gold,
Stories of life waiting to unfold.
As twilight dances, dreams take flight,
In the heart of stillness, we find our light.

When time entwines with peace so sweet,
The soul awakens, steady and complete.
In the hush of night, joy unfolds,
In solitude's arms, life's treasure holds.

Elysian Whispers in the Breeze

Across the meadow, whispers sweet,
In the wind's embrace, we find our beat.
With laughter swirling like petals in air,
Elysian dreams float everywhere.

Stars awaken as night descends,
With each soft murmur, our spirit blends.
Under celestial paths, we spin and twirl,
In the dance of the night, our hearts unfurl.

Glimmers of joy in the twilight glow,
A symphony of joy wrapped in the flow.
As shadows waltz with the light's soft kiss,
In elysian whispers, we find our bliss.

Together we weave this tapestry bright,
In the festival's glow, our spirits unite.
With every heartbeat, forever we seize,
In the elysian breeze, time gently flees.

Hues of an Unknown Tomorrow

Colors dance in joyous light,
Shadows fade as day turns bright.
Hopeful hearts begin to soar,
Waves of laughter, we want more.

Threads of dreams in radiant hues,
Painting skies, igniting views.
With each brush, a tale unfolds,
In every stroke, a future bold.

The Breeze that Tells No Lies

Whispers soft, the wind's embrace,
Carrying joy from place to place.
It twirls around, a playful tease,
Bringing warmth, a gentle breeze.

Laughter floats on wings of air,
Magic dances everywhere.
Every sigh, a sweet delight,
Chasing shadows, igniting light.

Beneath the Weight of Endless Sky

Stars that twinkle, dreams take flight,
Underneath the vast, clear night.
Gathered friends in harmony,
Singing songs of jubilee.

Infinite blue, a canvas wide,
Inviting hope with every tide.
We raise our cups to the bright moon,
In unison, our hearts attune.

Song of the Rolling Acres

Fields of green stretch far and wide,
Where the sun and laughter collide.
Bubbling brooks sing sweetest tunes,
Beneath the glow of glowing moons.

In the distance, children play,
Echoing joy in a perfect array.
Life's a melody, pure and free,
In rolling acres, bliss we see.

The Forgotten Meadow

In the meadow where wildflowers bloom,
Colors dance in joy, dispelling gloom.
Butterflies flit in the warm sunlight,
Every petal whispers a tale of delight.

Children's laughter on the playful breeze,
Nature's symphony played among the trees.
A canvas of dreams, so bright and free,
In this forgotten place, we find harmony.

Echoes of the Emptiness

In the stillness, a quiet cheer,
Memories linger, the past feels near.
Echoes of laughter, soft and sweet,
Bind our hearts in this rhythmic beat.

Under the stars, we gather round,
Whispers of joy in the night abound.
The moonlight dances, a silvery veil,
In the emptiness, our spirits sail.

Unseen Horizons

On the edge where hope meets the sky,
Dreams awaken and spirits fly.
Colors blend as twilight weaves,
A tapestry of wonder that never leaves.

Paths unknown call out our names,
In the adventure, nothing remains.
With laughter, we step into the night,
In unseen horizons, our hearts take flight.

Beneath the Silent Canopy

Beneath the branches, shadows play,
A tranquil moment at the close of day.
Whispers of nature, soft and low,
Carry tales from long ago.

Fireflies twinkle like stars in our hands,
As we build dreams on this enchanted land.
In the silence, we find a spark,
Beneath the canopy, we light the dark.

When the World Stands Still

Beneath the stars so bright, we stand,
With laughter shared, a warm command.
The world outside, a distant hum,
In our hearts, the beat of drum.

Candles flicker, shadows dance,
In this moment, we take a chance.
Joyful voices weave through the air,
In perfect harmony, without a care.

Time pauses, just for us tonight,
In every glance, pure delight.
Festive songs fill up the sky,
As we whisper dreams, you and I.

With every cheer, the night grows bright,
Together we hold the spirit tight.
When the world stands still, we find,
The magic we share, love intertwined.

Serenade of Rustling Leaves

Golden hues wrap the trees,
Whispers echo in the breeze.
Autumn's charm, a soft embrace,
A serenade in nature's grace.

Dancing leaves in swirls of cheer,
Nature's song, so bright and clear.
Children laughing, running free,
Underneath the old oak tree.

Picnics spread on checkered cloth,
Delicious treats, joy's warm froth.
Every bite, a shared delight,
As day surrenders into night.

Fires crackle, stories unfold,
In this warmth, together we hold.
The serenade of rustling leaves,
Is a treasure the heart believes.

Reflections on the Canvas of Earth

Each sunrise paints a tale anew,
On earth's canvas, vibrant hue.
Brushstrokes of joy, splashes of light,
A masterpiece born from day to night.

Fields of flowers in radiant bloom,
Swaying gently, dispelling gloom.
Nature dances, a festive display,
As we wander, carefree, and gay.

Rivers glisten in golden rays,
A mirror to life, it plays.
Collecting whispers of dreams we share,
Reflections of hope floating in air.

In every sunset, spirits rise,
The canvas unfolds, a sweet surprise.
Reflections beckon us to play,
In the gallery of the everyday.

Twilight in the Cornfields

Twilight falls on golden grains,
A hush envelops the plains.
Fireflies dance, igniting the dark,
Nature's way to leave a spark.

Children chase as shadows grow,
Laughter echoes, soft and low.
The air is sweet, a gentle thrill,
As joy wraps us like a warm quilt.

In the distance, a banjo strums,
Tales of old, sweetly hums.
With every note, hearts align,
Underneath the starry vine.

Together we gather, hearts aglow,
In this moment, time moves slow.
Twilight in the cornfields warm,
A cherished peace, a joyful charm.

Solace of the Twilight Hour

The sun dips low, a golden hue,
Soft whispers dance in skies so blue.
Laughter echoes in the fields,
As evening's calm slowly yields.

Fireflies flicker, a gentle light,
Families gather, hearts feel bright.
Songs of joy in the cooling air,
In twilight's grasp, all worries bare.

Cupcakes sweet with sprinkles bright,
Children's laughter, pure delight.
Stars begin their twinkling show,
In the solace, hearts aglow.

With friends beside, the night unfolds,
In tales retold, new bonds we mold.
As twilight whispers, dreams take flight,
In this brief pause, all feels right.

The Essence of Eroding Seasons

Leaves are falling, crisp and gold,
Stories of the year unfold.
Pumpkin patches, cider's steam,
In autumn's arms, we find our dream.

Family feasts with laughter shared,
Gratitude fills hearts laid bare.
The harvest moon shines in delight,
Celebrating life, at dusk's soft light.

Bonfires crackle, embers fly,
People gather, spirits high.
Traditions blend in warmth alive,
In every hug, we feel the thrive.

Through the seasons, memories weave,
In this essence, we believe.
As nature shifts, we find our place,
In every ending, we embrace.

Threads of Nature's Narrative

In the forest, whispers play,
Nature's tales greet every day.
Rustling leaves and bubbling streams,
Echoes of a poet's dreams.

Colors shift in vibrant dance,
Every petal, a fleeting chance.
The sunbeams kiss as flowers bloom,
Creating soft, fragrant rooms.

Deer wander through the golden glade,
In shadows deep, and light's parade.
Stories linger in each breeze,
Awakening hearts with gentle ease.

So let us roam where wild things sing,
In joy and nature's offering.
With every thread, a tale to tell,
In nature's arms, we dwell so well.

Recollections in a Fledgling Breeze

A breeze whispers secrets untold,
Of summer's warmth and joys of old.
Memories flow like a gentle stream,
In the light of dusk, where we dream.

Picnics spread on grassy fields,
Laughter shines, and friendship yields.
Kites soar high, painted skies,
In every heart, a spark that flies.

As stars awaken, fireflies gleam,
In every flicker, a hopeful dream.
Together we cherish the night's embrace,
In the fleeting time, we find our pace.

With nature close and love profound,
In this moment, our joy is found.
The fledgling breeze carries our song,
In memory's arms, forever strong.

Reverie in the Open Air

Beneath the sky so wide and blue,
Laughter dances like morning dew,
Colors twirl in a merry play,
Joyous whispers fill the day.

Breezes carry sweet perfume,
As blossoms burst in joyful bloom,
Children chase with cheerful glee,
While sunshine warms the festive spree.

In every heart, a song does rise,
Underneath the brightened skies,
Hope and laughter intertwine,
In this moment, all is fine.

Evening falls with amber glow,
As stars awaken soft and slow,
The world transforms in light's embrace,
A night of dreams in this special place.

Beyond the Reeds and Wind

Where willow branches gently sway,
The sun spills gold on water's play,
Picnics shared on grass so green,
In this haven, joy is seen.

Lively whispers in the breeze,
Dance of leaves upon the trees,
Children spin with hearts so light,
Painting wishes, pure delight.

Laughter flows like rivers wide,
In the warm and flowing tide,
As friends gather, spirits soar,
Sharing dreams forevermore.

Magic glows as dusk descends,
Wrapping all in warmth it sends,
With a toast to nights so bright,
Together we chase the light.

Silhouettes of Untouched Greens

In the twilight, shadows bloom,
Nature's beauty, life's perfume,
Mountains stand with peaks so grand,
Calling all to explore the land.

Fields of gold beneath the sun,
A whispering song for everyone,
Giggling streams and laughter near,
In this space, we shed our fear.

Over hills, the skylarks sing,
Tales of joy the echoes bring,
Dancing hearts in vibrant hues,
Painting life with festive views.

As stars ignite the velvet sky,
We share our dreams, let spirits fly,
In the night, our souls unite,
In this peace, our hearts take flight.

The Lure of Distant Landscapes

Horizons stretch beyond the view,
Adventures wait in every hue,
A call to wander and explore,
To find what lies on distant shore.

Candles flicker in the night,
Casting warmth, a sacred light,
Stories shared with laughter bright,
In this realm, all feels right.

Echoes of a festive cheer,
As friends gather, drawing near,
With every toast and joyful song,
We celebrate where hearts belong.

The moon above, a guiding flame,
Uniting all, no two the same,
In every smile, a spark ignites,
Illuminating joyful nights.

Memories of Green in Grey

In fields of whispers, where colors play,
The laughter dances, chasing grey away.
With every heartbeat, the joy flows bright,
In the tapestry woven, dreams take flight.

Breezes carry tales of summers past,
Moments like dewdrops, fading fast.
Yet in each corner, a spark remains,
Memories of green, untouched by pains.

Underneath the skies that softly glow,
The vibrant echoes of the love we know.
Wrapped in the warmth of a sunlit cheer,
We gather the moments, forever near.

So let the laughter echo through the trees,
In this festive spirit, our hearts can seize.
For even in shadows, the light can beam,
Memories of green, forever our dream.

Where the Wildflowers Whisper

In meadows blooming with colors bright,
Where wildflowers whisper, pure delight.
A symphony played by the gentle breeze,
Each petal sways and dances with ease.

Under the sun's warmth, the world transforms,
Nature's palette bursts with lively forms.
Laughter spills over like a river's flow,
Painting joy across the land we know.

With every step on this vibrant ground,
The secrets of wild blooms can be found.
In this festive realm, our hearts unite,
Together we bask in spring's soft light.

So let the wildflowers sing their song,
In this lush haven, we all belong.
With smiles as bright as the sun's warm rays,
We'll cherish these moments, countless days.

Secrets Beneath the Sun

Under the sky, we chase the light,
Collecting secrets, spirits feel so bright.
With every shadow, a story unfolds,
In laughter and love, the heart boldly holds.

The sun paints us golden, a radiant hue,
In the festive dance, we feel the new.
Whispers of friendship float on the air,
Together we weave a bond so rare.

With glimmers of joy each moment brings,
The world comes alive as our laughter sings.
Among the blossoms, life blooms anew,
In every heartbeat, our dreams shine through.

So let's celebrate all that we are,
With dreams in our pockets, we're never far.
In the warmth of the sun, our spirits run free,
Embracing the magic of you and me.

Beyond the Golden Grain

In fields of gold, where harvests gleam,
We gather our blessings, and dance in a dream.
The wind carries laughter, crisp and clear,
In this festive season, we hold dear.

With every rustle, the stories call,
Of friendship and love that conquer all.
The grains sway gently, a rhythmic song,
Inviting us to where we all belong.

Beneath the vast sky, we lift our hands,
Celebrating together, in life's grand plans.
With joyful hearts, we embrace the day,
In unity's warmth, we laugh and play.

So let the golden grains remind us well,
Of moments shared and stories to tell.
In the beauty of harvest, joy intertwines,
Beyond the golden grain, life brightly shines.

Lullabies of an Empty Farmstead

In fields where silence softly lays,
The moonlight dances, bright and gay.
Crickets sing their evening charms,
As dreams embrace the night's warm arms.

The old barn creaks a gentle tune,
Under the watch of silver moon.
Whispers float on autumn breeze,
Awakening the memories of trees.

Stars twinkle like a fanciful kite,
Painting the darkness with glittering light.
Old shadows waltz across the land,
Kissed by the touch of a gentle hand.

With every breeze, a tale unfolds,
Of laughter shared in days of gold.
The farmstead hums a lullaby,
While tranquil night embraces sky.

Echoing Dreams of Celestial Meadows

In meadows where the daisies sway,
Colors burst in joyful play.
Butterflies dance in radiant hues,
Painting the air with blissful views.

Whispers of spring in every bloom,
Chasing away the winter's gloom.
The laughter of children fills the air,
As they weave dreams without a care.

Clouds drift by in a gentle race,
Mirroring smiles on every face.
The sun dips low with warm embrace,
Kissing the earth in a sweet grace.

Echoes of joy in twilight linger,
Fingers trace the stars like a singer.
As night descends, stories are spun,
Under the gaze of the infinite sun.

Whispers Beyond the Horizon

Beyond the hills where shadows play,
Whispers travel and fade away.
Golden sunsets wrap the day,
In soft embrace, they gently sway.

The laughter of friends, a treasured sound,
Echoes softly from the ground.
Wishballoons hover in twilight's grasp,
As dreams drift on with an eager clasp.

Stars awaken, a dazzling show,
Guiding hearts where wishes flow.
The night's gentle breath whispers low,
Painting the world in silver glow.

As moonbeams weave through trees so high,
The world spins softly, a lullaby.
Each whisper tells of dreams anew,
Carried forth on skies so blue.

Chasing Shadows at Twilight

As daylight fades with a gentle sigh,
Shadows play as the night drifts by.
Children's laughter in the cooling air,
Chasing whispers without a care.

Fireflies light up the darkening scene,
Flickers of magic, soft and serene.
The horizon blushes in shades of gold,
While stories of old are lovingly told.

Cool breezes dance through fields of green,
Rustling softly, a peaceful glean.
The stars awake, one by one,
Winking down at a day well done.

With every shadow that fades away,
A new adventure begins to play.
As twilight wraps the world so tight,
We chase the dreams into the night.

Remnants of a Wandering Heart

In twilight's dance, we gather near,
With laughter bright, and hearts sincere.
A tapestry of dreams unfolds,
As stories of our paths are told.

The stars align, like sparks of gold,
In memories, our tales are rolled.
Each step we take, a note of cheer,
In festive nights that draw us near.

The melodies weave through the air,
With whispers soft that we all share.
A wandering heart finds solace sweet,
In every smile, in every greet.

So let us feast, and joyously sing,
Embrace the warmth that laughter brings.
For in this moment, life is art,
We celebrate the wandering heart.

The Lark's Soliloquy

A lark takes flight with morning's glow,
In fields of green where wild dreams flow.
Its song of joy, a sweet refrain,
That lifts our spirits, free of pain.

With every note, the world awakes,
The heart rejoices, and the earth shakes.
A symphony of life begins,
As laughter dances on the winds.

Beneath a sky of azure light,
We celebrate this pure delight.
Together here, in festive cheer,
We find our joy in every year.

So let the lark's sweet song resound,
Encircling us, as joy is found.
In every heart, let music stay,
As we embrace this festive day.

Mist Over Ancient Pastures

Amidst the mist, where shadows play,
Ancient pastures welcome the day.
With echoes of the past to cheer,
We dance in joy, as memories near.

The sun breaks through, a golden hue,
As laughter mingles with the dew.
A tapestry of life unfolds,
In every tale that time upholds.

We raise our glasses to the skies,
With every cheer, our spirits rise.
In fields where dreams and memories meet,
We gather here, our hearts complete.

So let the mist weave stories bright,
In festive rhythms, pure delight.
For in this hour, we feel the past,
With every smile, a bond that's cast.

Dreaming in Shades of Amber

In twilight's glow, the world transforms,
As amber hues take on new forms.
We dream beneath the starlit sky,
With laughter echoing, spirits high.

The warmth of candles lights our way,
In moments shared, we choose to stay.
Each whisper soft, like tender song,
In festive hearts, we all belong.

The night unfolds, a canvas wide,
With joy and love that cannot hide.
In every twinkle, every glance,
We drift and sway, caught in this dance.

So let us weave our dreams anew,
In shades of amber, bright and true.
With every heartbeat, let us sing,
In festive spirits, everlasting.

Glimpses of an Endless Expanse

Balloons float high, colors bright,
Laughter dances in soft light.
Joyful hearts in a merry spree,
Life feels sweet, wild, and free.

Candles flicker as night falls,
Whispers echo through the halls.
The air is thick with cheer and sound,
A warm embrace all around.

Fireworks burst in vivid flair,
Shimmering sparks fill the air.
Under the stars, dreams take flight,
In this moment, all feels right.

Together we share this blissful night,
With friends and family, spirits delight.
Through smiles and hugs, our bonds will grow,
In glimpses of love, we overflow.

Dreams Carried by the Breeze

Kites soar high, tracing the sky,
Colors vivacious, laughter close by.
Children chase dreams, feet dancing light,
With each breeze, hearts take flight.

Picnics spread on a sunlit shore,
Lemonade flowing, we crave more.
Songs intertwine with the gentle air,
Each note a promise, a joyful affair.

Footsteps on paths of golden grain,
Whispers of magic in the plain.
Under the shade of an old oak tree,
We find our peace, we feel so free.

Breezes carry our stories far,
Like wishes sent to a distant star.
In every moment, joy is seized,
As we follow dreams carried by the breeze.

Sowing Seeds in Far-off Dreams

In the garden, laughter blooms,
Nature dances, chasing glooms.
With each seed, hopes are sown,
In the sunlight, love is grown.

Children gather, hands in dirt,
They uncover joy, and mirth.
Tiny flowers break through the ground,
In every petal, beauty found.

Whispers shared beneath the trees,
Stories float on a gentle breeze.
Each moment cherished, laughter beams,
As we sow the seeds of dreams.

The harvest glows in golden light,
Bound by love, we hold on tight.
With every flower, our hearts expand,
Sowing seeds in far-off lands.

Where the Sky Meets the Plains

Golden fields stretch far and wide,
Under the sun, where dreams reside.
With every breath, freedom reigns,
In the vastness where sky meets plains.

Dancing shadows in the late sun,
Whispering winds, our hearts run.
The horizon glimmers with promise bright,
As day surrenders to the night.

Bonfires crackle, stories unfold,
In warm tones, the night is bold.
Friendship ties with the flicker's glow,
In this moment, we all know.

Where laughter lingers and spirits rise,
Together we bask in joyful ties.
At the edge where the wild remains,
We find ourselves where sky meets plains.

www.ingramcontent.com/pod-product-compliance
Ingram Content Group UK Ltd.
Pitfield, Milton Keynes, MK11 3LW, UK
UKHW030848221224
452712UK00006B/429